FRANKISH & VISIGOTHIC COUNCILS

Translated by: D.P. Curtin

FRANKISH & VISIGOTHIC COUNCILS

Copyright @ 2007 Dalcassian Publishing Company

All rights reserved. No part of this publication may be reproduced, distributed, or transmitted in any form or by any means, including photocopying, recording, or other electronic or mechanical methods, without the prior written permission of the publisher, except in the case of brief quotations embodied in critical reviews and certain other non-commercial uses permitted by copyright law. For permission request, write to Dalcassian Publishing Company at dalcassianpublishing at gmail.com

ISBN: 979-8-8691-0860-9 (Paperback)

Library of Congress Control Number:
Author: Curtin, D.P. (1985-)

Printed by Ingram Content Group, 1 Ingram Blvd, La Vergne, Tennessee

First printing edition 2007.

FRANKISH & VISIGOTHIC COUNCILS

5th Council of Orleans (549 AD)
under St. Sacerdos of Lyon

1. Condemnation of the errors of Eutyches and Nestorius.

2. No bishop must excommunicate a faithful on insufficient grounds.

3. No bishop, priest or deacon must have a wife in his home, and even women who are related to him must not be in his house at odd hours.

4. When a cleric, of whatever degree he is, returns to married life, he must, throughout his life, be removed from the catalog of clerics (*ab honore accepti ordinis*) and stripped of his functions (*ab officio*); no house must grant him communion.

5. No bishop shall promote a foreign cleric or reader, or take him for himself, without the consent of the cleric's bishop; if he does so, he must remain six months without saying mass, and the cleric thus promoted will be, according to the judgment of his own bishop, suspended.

6. No bishop shall ordain a slave or a freedman without the consent of his master or of the one who freed him. If he does so, he will be six months without saying mass, and whoever he has ordained will have to return to his master; however, he must treat him in accordance with his (ecclesiastical) state. If this

master does not do it, the bishop must give him two other slaves, and ask for his church the one who has been ordained.

7. When slaves have been freed by their masters in churches, the Church must defend their freedom.

8. When a bishop dies in a city, no other bishop must, before the see is reoccupied, ordain clerics in that city, nor in the parishes, nor consecrate altars, or take anything from the property of the Church.

9. No layman should be ordained by a bishop unless a year has passed since his conversion. During this time, he must be carefully instructed in ecclesiastical discipline and rules by learned and proven men.
10. No one must buy a bishopric, nor obtain it with the help of gifts; but any new bishop must be elected by the clergy and by the people, in accordance with the ancient canons, and have the assent of the king; he will be consecrated by the metropolitan, or by his replacement, and in union with the other bishops of province.

10. Whoever buys a bishopric or is ordained for gifts will be deposed.

11. A bishop should not be imposed on a parish (diocese) which it does not want, and the laity and clergy should not be forced by the powerful to adhere to (such an intrusion). The bishop thus enthroned by force will forever lose the episcopal dignity.

12. No bishop should be given a successor during his lifetime nor should another bishop be placed on his seat unless he has been deposed for a capital offense.

13. No one must keep, alienate or subtract what has been given to churches, convents, hospitals; if he does so, he must, in accordance with the ancient canons, be excluded from the Church as a murderer of the poor, until he has returned what he took.

14. No bishop, no cleric, and in general no one should seize the property of another Church, nor receive it.

15. As regards the Xenodockium founded in Lyon by King Childebert I and his wife Ultrogothe, the bishop of this city must not claim for himself or for his church any of the property attributed to him. Anyone who infringes on the rights or property of this Xenodockium will be irrevocably anathema as a murderer of the poor.

16. He who wants to take back what he himself or his ancestors gave to priests and churches, or to any other consecrated place, must be excommunicated, as a murderer of the poor.

17. Whoever has a conflict with a bishop or with a steward of Church property, must first seek to settle the matter amicably. If he doesn't succeed, he should contact the metropolitan. If the bishop, thus put on notice, does not satisfy his adversaries, after a double exhortation from his metropolitan, and if he does not appear before this metropolitan, he will be excluded from the fraternal communion (a charitate) of the metropolitan, until he appears and explains himself on this debate. If it is proven that he is in the right, the one who brought this false accusation will be excommunicated for one year. But if the metropolitan has been twice asked by one of the bishops of his province to take care of a matter, and if he does not do so, the bishop must refer his matter to the next synod and comply with the decision of his co-provincials.

18. Renewal of the 19th canon of the second council of Arles

19. Young girls who voluntarily enter a monastery, or who are offered there by their parents, must keep, for one year, the habit they had on their entry. If it is a monastery where they are not perpetually recluse, they will wear for three years the habit that they brought with them, and only after this time will they take the dress of the order. If they later go out and marry, they and their husbands will be excommunicated. If they separate, they can be admitted to communion again.

20. The archdeacon or provost of the church must visit, every Sunday, the prisoners, so that their misery may be, according to the commandment of God, alleviated by mercy. The bishop must appoint a faithful and hard-working person to take care of the needs of the prisoners. The bishop will cover the necessary costs.

FRANKISH & VISIGOTHIC COUNCILS

21. The bishop must take particular care of lepers, and ensure that they have something to wear and eat:

22. If a guilty slave has taken refuge in a church (as in an asylum), he must, in accordance with the ancient ordinances, not be returned until his master has promised by oath to forgive him. If the master does not keep his promise, and persecutes this slave, he will be excluded from all relations with the faithful. If, the master having taken this oath, the slave does not want to leave the church, his master can force him out. If the master is a pagan or a stranger to the church, he must take, as guarantors of the promise of forgiveness made to the slave, several people of recognized piety.

23. A provincial council must be held every year.

24. The ancient canons retain the force of law.

> Sacerdos of Lyon
> Aurelianus of Arles
> Eutychius of Vienne
> Nicerius of Trier
> Desiderius of Bourges
> Aspasius of Elusa
> Constitutus of Sens
> Placidus of Mâcon
> Firminus of Uzès
> Agricola of Chalon-sur-Saône
> Urbicus of Bazas
> Rufus of Valence
> Gallus of Auvergne
> Saffaracus of Paris
> Domitianus of Tungrensis
> Eleutherius of Auxerre
> Desiderius of Verdun
> Grammatius of Laon
> Tetricus of Langres
>
> Nectarius of Autun
> Eusebius of Saintes
> Proculeianus of Auch
> Maximus of Cahors
> Bebianus of Agen
> Aptonius of Angouleme
> Deuterius of Vence
> Lauto of Coutances
> Passivus of Séez
> Clematius of Carpentras
> Vellesius of Gap
> Aregius of Nevers
> Hilarius of Digne
> Clementius of Apt
> Palladius of Toulon
> Basilius of Glandèves
> Avolus of Aix
> Febediolus of Rennes
> Gallus of Valence
> Leubenus of Chartres
> Theudobaudis of Lisieux

Alodius of Tulle
Licinius of Évreux
Medoveus of Meaux
Liberius of Dax
Amelius of Comminges
Aletius of Leictoure
Gonotigernus of Senlis
Aegridius of Avranches
Beatus of Amiens
Ambrosius of Saint-Paul-trois-Châteaux
Antoninus of Avignon
Magnus of Nice and Cimies
Melanus of Albi
Lucretius of Die
Pappulus of Geneva
Leucadius of Bayeux
Faustus of Riez
Expectatus of Fréjus
Eusebius of Antibes
Praetextatus of Châlons-sur-Saône
Vindemialis of Orange
Gallicanus of Embrun
Agrestius of Tours
Leontius of Bordeaux
Avolus of Sisteron
Ruricius of Limoges
Ambrosius of Albi
Theodorus of Conserans
Mappinius of Reims
Gennobaudus of Lugdunum
Albinus of Angers

Council of Auch (551 AD)
under St. Aspasius of Auch

1. Whoever, after receiving penitence, is proved to have returned to his wives, as if he had been thrown out, or to others, even if it is known that he has joined himself unlawfully with a manly woman, let them know that he has been abducted both from communion and from the limits of the Church or the feast of Catholics.

2. If indeed any bishop, priest, or deacon, in addition to these persons whom the holy synod has decreed to be in the comfort of the clergy, should perhaps presume to have with him a woman who is not a stranger, or if he wishes to have the secret of the cellar, both virgin and maidservant, for any familiarity, he shall deposit all the sacerdotal sacrifice removing himself from the thresholds of the holy Church or from every meeting of the Catholics let him be struck by the order of the aforesaid synod.

3. Concerning enchanters, or those who are said to incantate the devil's horns by instinct, if the superior persons happen to be sued, they are driven from the thresholds by excommunication to the church, but the humbler persons or servants are reprimanded by the judge, so that if they hide themselves from being corrected by the fear of God, as it is written, they must be corrected with lashes.

4. But it is the business of the priests, or of all the clerics, that they should not exercise their activities with the laity, but with their co-provincial bishops, if the holy synod araussically precepts should be kept for that reason, so that if anyone despises the above written precepts, excommunication of all this detestation is considered worthy; likewise, if he had fled to the patronage of a layman in contempt of his pontiff, when he had been rebuked by his bishop and the layman wished to defend him, the same penalty of excommunication was inflicted upon them.

5. As regards the ordination of clerics, it is agreed that when a priest or a deacon is asked to be ordained by the bishop, in the days preceding the wine, the people should know that someone is to be ordained, and if by any chance he knows that there is harm to him from among the people, he should not stop saying the ordination before the ordination 4 ; so that, if no one is about to issue a certain disapproval, he may without any hesitation accept the benediction that he deserves to be inspected.

6. If, however, as a remedy for evil, he has taken care to offer such mancipia or sacred places to churches or monasteries, then, as the one who donated it has written, it is to be observed in all things, as well as to the families of the church, with the understanding of piety and the justice that is appropriate to be observed as the family of God, as much lighter The servants of private persons should be kept in labor, so that they may rejoice that the fourth tribute or any of their work, blessing God, has been granted to them as priests from the present time.

7. For, as the precepts of our holy fathers declare, once a year the holy assembly of the bishops gathers together in their places, it is especially fitting to observe it. Feb. in the 40th year of the reign of our lord Childibert I (King of Paris) and Chlothar I (King of Soissons).

>   Aspasius, archbishop of Auch
>   Julien, bishop of Bigorre
>   Proculejanus of Auch
>   Liberius, bishop of Acqs
>   Theodore, bishop of Conserans

Amelius, bishop of Cominges, *and three other suffragans, of whom we do not know the seats.*

5th Council of Arles (554 AD)
under Sapaudus, bishop of Arles

1. All bishops of the province are ordered to follow, under penalty of exclusion 'acommunione velacharitale fratrum', the practice followed by the Metropolitan Church of Arles regarding offerings.

2. Monasteries and the government of monks come under the jurisdiction of the bishop in whose diocese the monastery is located.

3. No abbot must, without the permission of his bishop, be absent from his monastery for a long time. Otherwise, he will be punished by this bishop s,

4. No priest shall depose a deacon or subdeacon without the knowledge of the bishop. If he does so, the one who has been deposed will be received again into communion, and the one who has pronounced the deposition will himself be excommunicated for a year.

5. The bishop must take care of the nuns who are in his city, and the abbess must not do anything against the rules.

6. Clerics must not damage church property entrusted to them by the bishop; if they do, the younger ones (those who are not subdeacons) will be punished, and the older ones will be treated as murderers of the poor.

7. No bishop shall ordain a foreign cleric without a letter from that cleric's bishop; if he does so, the one who has been ordained will lose the dignity received [ab honore quem acceperit remotus] and will not be able to carry out the functions entrusted to him, and the one who has made the ordination will, for three months, excluded from communion.

3rd Council of Paris (557 AD)
under St. Germain, bishop of Paris

1. Whoever illegally possesses and keeps the property of the Church must be excommunicated until he recognizes his guilt. Such people are murderers of the poor. Before punishing them, the bishop must send them an official warning, so that the unjust holder of the Church's property can return it. If he refuses and it is necessary to use coercion, the thief will receive prompt punishment; in order to keep property of the Church, no one must, under penalty of excommunication, pretend that this property is in another kingdom (than the church to which it belongs), because the power of God knows no limits . No one shall keep church property, under the pretext that it was previously given to him by the king; the bishops, relying on the canons, should have long ago spoken out against such people; They decided to do it now that they were ruined by the damage they had had to suffer. If the unjust holder of Church property resides in another diocese, the bishop (whose property he unjustly owns) must inform the other bishop, so that the latter can remonstrate with the guilty party, or punishes him with canonical penalties; If in the past, in times of trouble, someone seized the goods of the Church with the permission of King Clovis, of blessed memory, and left them to his children, they must return them. The bishops must not only preserve the founding documents, they must also effectively defend the assets of Éolise.

2. We must also punish, as thieves of the Church's property, those who harm the bishop's property.

3. No bishop must own property that does not belong to him; if he has any, he must return it without pretending that the king gave it to him.

4. Incestuous marriages are prohibited; it is forbidden to marry the widow of the brother, the mother-in-law, the widow of an uncle (brother of the father or the mother), the sister of one's own wife, the daughter-in-law, the aunt (sister of the father or of the mother), the daughter-in-law or the daughter of the latter.

5. No one shall marry a virgin consecrated to God, either by kidnapping or by marriage proposal. Likewise, it is forbidden, under penalty of perpetual excommunication, to marry those who, having left the clothes of the world, have taken a vow of emptiness or virginity.

6. No one should ask the king for anything that does not belong to him. It is forbidden to all, under penalty of excommunication, to obtain from the king, or to kidnap a widow or a daughter whose parents do not want to give.

7. No bishop should receive one who has been excommunicated by another bishop.

8. We must not impose on a city a bishop who has not been freely elected by the people and by the clergy. He must not be enthroned by order of the prince, or in any other way, against the will of the metropolitan or the other bishops of the province. If anyone, citing an order from the king, dares to seize such a high position, he will not be received by the other bishops of the province. If a bishop of the province enters into contact with him, he will be excluded from the communion of his colleagues. Concerning these authorizations, the metropolitan, assisted by the bishops of the province, or other neighboring bishops chosen by him, will decide on their value, after having deliberated jointly.

9. The descendants of slaves designated to fulfill certain offices at the tombs of their deceased masters must fulfill the conditions of their emancipation with the greatest fidelity; whether it is the heirs or the Church who are responsible for ensuring this. In the event that the Church has completely released them from their royalties vis-à-vis the tax authorities, they must, themselves and their descendants, remain constantly under the protection of the Church and pay the tribute for this protection.

10. These ordinances will be presented for the signature of the absent bishops.

1st Council of Braga (561 AD)
under Lucretius, archbishop of Braga

1. Whoever does not profess that the Father, the Son and the Holy Spirit are three persons of one substance, or force or power, as the Catholic and Apostolic Church teaches, but on the contrary maintains that he there is only one person, so that he who is the Son is also the Father and the Paraclete, as Sabellius and Priscillian taught, let him be anathema.

2. Whoever, disregarding the Holy Trinity, introduces new names to designate the divinity, maintaining that there is in the divinity a trinity of the trinity, as the Gnostics and Priscillianists teach, let him be anathema.

3. Whoever says that the Son of God Our Lord did not exist before his birth from Mary, as Paul of Samosata, Photinus and Priscillian taught, let him be anathema.

4. Whoever does not honor the day of Christ's birth, but fasts on that day, as well as on Sunday, because he believes that Christ was not born with a true human nature, as does the taught Cerdon, Marcion, Manes and Priscillian, let him be anathema.

5. Whoever believes that the souls of men and the angels are born from the substance of God, as Manes and Priscillian maintained, let him be anathema.

6. Whoever says that the souls of men originally sinned in heaven, and were therefore sent to earth in the bodies of men, as Priscillian taught, let him be anathema.

7. Whoever denies that the demon was in the beginning a good angel created by God, and maintains that the demon was formed from chaos and darkness, that he has no creator, but is himself, even the principle and substance of evil, as Manes and Priscillian taught, let it be anathema.

8. Whoever believes that because the devil brought certain things to the earth, he made thunder, lightning, storm and drought by his own power, as Priscillian taught, let him be anathema.

9. Whoever believes that the souls and bodies of men are subject to the course of the stars, as the pagans and Priscillian taught, let him be anathema.

10. Whoever believes that the twelve signs (of the Zodiac) ordinarily observed by mathematicians are divided according to the parts of the soul and the body, and are attributed to the names of the patriarchs, as Priscillian taught, let him be anathema.

11. Whoever condemns marriage and abhors generation, like Manes and Priscillian, let him be anathema.

12. Whoever says that the formation of the human body and conception in the womb of the woman is the work of the devil, and therefore does not believe in the resurrection of the flesh, as Manes and Priscillian maintained, let him be anathema.

13. Whoever says that the creation of the flesh is not, in general, the work of God, but that of evil angels, as Manes and Priscillian claimed, let him be anathema.

14. Whoever declares unclean the meats that God has given to man for his food, and abstains from eating them, not to punish the body, but because of this alleged impurity, and is content with vegetables prepared without meat, as Manes and Priscillian did, let him be anathema.

15. The cleric or monk who, with the exception of his mother, or his sister, or his aunt, or another close relative, adopts a woman, or keeps her in his home, or lives with her, as the sect of Priscillianists allows, will be anathema.

16. Whoever, on Maundy Thursday, does not attend mass, on an empty stomach, in the church, at a specified hour after none; but, following the custom of the sect of the Priscillianists, celebrate, from the third, the solemnity of this day, by interrupting the fast after having attended a mass of the dead, let him be anathema.

17. Whoever reads the holy Scriptures falsified by Priscillian according to his errors, or the treatises which Dictinius wrote before his conversion, or other books of the heretics, whether these claim to have been written by the patriarchs, the prophets or the apostles, and if he defends and accepts their impious fables, let him be anathema.

2nd Council of Lyon (567 AD)
under Pope John III of Rome

1. When, in an ecclesiastical province, a conflict has arisen between bishops, they must accept the decision of the metropolitan and the other bishops of the province. If the conflict takes place between bishops of different provinces, their metropolitans will decide. A bishop wronged by a colleague or another person must be defended by all his brothers.

2. What bishops or clerics have received by will cannot be taken away from them, even if the succession has not been made in accordance with civil laws. Anyone who touches such donations will be excluded from the communion of the faithful until restitution.

3. Whoever makes or wants to make a slave someone who has lived in peace for a long time without being worried about his status (as a free man), must be excommunicated until he desists.

4. He who has been excommunicated by a bishop must be treated as such by all other bishops, until the bishop who pronounced the excommunication believes the time has come to pardon the offender.

5. What bishops have given to some clerics, whether ecclesiastical property for enjoyment, or their own property in full ownership, must not be taken away later by other bishops. When clerics have sinned, the punishment must be

imposed on people according to their rank and in accordance with the canons, but it must not apply to property.

6. In the first week of the ninth month, before the first Sunday of this month, processions must be made in all the churches, as they take place, in accordance with the ordinances of the Fathers, before the Ascension.

Council of Tours (567 AD)
under Eufronius, bishop of Tours

1. There must be two provincial synods every year, or if, as has happened up to now, they cannot be held, it is important that there be one every year. Only in the case of illness, but not an order from the king, can exempt you from going there. If the bishop does not go there, he must be excluded from the communion of his colleagues until the next great council and no bishop from another province must not be in communion with him.

2. When conflicts arise between bishops, they must take priests (*presbyteros*) as arbiters and conciliators. Anyone who does not submit to the judgment passed by these arbiters and conciliators, freely chosen on both sides the other, must be punished by Council.

3. 'Ut corpus Domini in altari non in imaginario ordine, sed sub crucis titulo componatur'. Some translate: "The body of the Lord (that is to say the particles of the consecrated bread) must not be placed on the altar in any order, and according to the priest's fancy, but in the right form. cross". Others: "The body of the Lord must not be placed on the altar with the images, but it must be preserved in the interior of the cross.

4. Both at vigils and during mass, the laity must not be with the clerics near the altar on which the holy mysteries are celebrated; but there must be between the balustrade and the altar a place intended for the clerics who form the choir.

However, for prayer (that is to say for private prayer outside the divine service) and for communion, the Lay people can, just like women, and following tradition, enter the holy place (sancta sanctorum).

5. Every community must feed its poor, and the poor must not run here and there to foreign cities.

6. No cleric or layman should give letters (of recommendation); it only belongs to the bishop.

7. No bishop must depose an abbot or an archpriest without having taken advice from other abbots or priests.

8. When a bishop, knowing that someone has been excommunicated by another bishop, remains in communion with him, he himself will be excluded from communion until the next council.

9. In the province of Armorica no one must consecrate the bishop, no more a Breton than a Roman, without the assent of the metropolitan and the other bishops of the province, and this under penalty of exclusion from the communion of bishops until the next council.

10. No bishop, priest, deacon or subdeacon must have at home, to lead his house, any woman other than his mother, his sister or his daughter; he must not have a nun, nor a widow, nor a servant.

11. Every bishop must ensure compliance with the previous ordinance. The metropolitan must help the bishops of the province to observe it, and they must, for their part, help the metropolitan in this.

12. The bishop must treat his wife as his sister. Wherever he is, he must be surrounded by clerics, and his dwelling must be separated from that of his wife, so that the clerics who serve the bishop are not in contact with the servants of the bishop's wife.

13. A bishop who does not have a wife (*episcopani*) must not have a wife in his retinue, and the clerics who serve him have the right to expel women from the bishop's house.

14. No priest or monk should sleep with another in the same bed, in order to avoid all suspicion; the monks must not live alone, or in two clans in separate cells, but they must all sleep together in a single schoia, under the supervision of the abbot or the provost. For this two or three, in turn, must watch and read, while the others rest.

15. Anyone who has entered a convent must no longer leave it and marry. If he does so, he will be excommunicated; and, if necessary, the assistance of civil authority will be used to separate him from his wife. If the judge refuses his assistance for this, he will be also excommunicated; he who defends a monk soiled with such an offense will himself be excommunicated, until the monk returns to his monastery and does the penance inflicted by his abbot.

16. No woman should visit a religious man; the abbot who suffers it will be excommunicated.

17. Regarding the fasting of monks, the ancient ordinance will be observed. From Easter until Pentecost, the monks will be served every day with the exception of Rogation days, a prandium (lunch which took place around noon, and before the end). After Pentecost, they must fast a whole week, and then, until August 1st, they fast three days a week, Monday, Wednesday and Friday, however with the exception of the sick. In the month of August we will give prandium every day, because there are *misse sanctorum* every day (and not holidays). In the months of September, October, and November, one must again fast three times a week, and in December one must fast every day until Christmas. From Christmas to Epiphany, prandium will be given every day, because all days are feast days. However, we will accept the three days of January, for which the holy Fathers have ordered special litanies, in order to combat pagan customs. On January 1, the day of the feast of the Circumcision, mass must be sung at eight o'clock. From Epiphany to Lent, we will fast three times a week 4.

18. In honor of Saint Martin, we must, both in his church and in others, follow the following order for psalmody: in summer we must sing at matins six antiphones with each two psalms; during the month of August there will be the manicationes i because in this month are the feasts and masses of the saints; in

September there will be seven antiphones with two psalms each, in October eight antiphones with three psalms each, in November nine antiphones with three psalms each, in December ten antiphones with three psalms each; there will be as many in January and February until Easter, more or less as possible. However, there must not be less than twelve psalms at matins as well as six at sext, and twelve at the twelfth hour, with the alleluia. Whoever has said less than twelve psalms at matins must fast until evening, and then have only bread and water. He will not be able to eat until the next day.

19. As a very large number of archpriests living in the countryside, as well as deacons and subdeacons, are accused of continuing to live with their wives, the archpriest must when he is in the city or when he goes in his countryside to have with him a clerk who follows him everywhere, and who has his bed in the same room as him. Seven subdeacons, or readers or lay people can alternate to exercise this supervision, they will take turns per week, anyone who evades this will be castigated. If the priest is negligent in carrying out this practice, he will be deprived of communion for thirty days until, having done penance, he returns to grace. The other priests, deacons and subdeacons living the countryside must take care that their slaves (women) live constantly where their own women are; as for them, they must remain alone in their cell and pray there. When a priest lives with his priestess (his wife), the deacon with his deacon, the subdeacon with his subdeaconess, he will be excommunicated for one year, and stripped forever of his ecclesiastical functions; he will return to secular life. He will only be able to sing among the readers. Archpriests who do not watch over the young clerics entrusted to them and do not take measures in this regard must be locked up in a cell in the city where they reside and live there for a month on bread and water. and do penance for the clerics entrusted to them. The people must not revere, but despise the priest who lives with his wife: because instead of being a doctor of penitence, he is a doctor of libertinage.

20. Virgins who have taken the veil, and widows who have taken vows must no longer, under penalty of excommunication, marry. One must not pretend that a virgin has not taken the habit (the veil) only in order not to be forced to contract a disadvantageous marriage: because the kings Childebert, Clotaire and Charibert decreed that no one should seize a young girl despite the will of her parents. If a virgin fears that 'violence is done to her, so that she takes refuge

in the church, until her parents can deliver her; she will then be able to marry; but if she changes her clothes, she must persist in her resolution. Concerning widows, we must not say that they can remarry, because they have not been blessed; it is true that it is forbidden to bless them; but their wishes are no less valid.

21. The ancient canons concerning incestuous marriages must retain the force of law.

22. Some, continuing their old wanderings, celebrate January 1; others bring food to the dead for the feast of the Siege of Peter and eat vegetables offered to the demon; others worship certain rocks, or trees, springs, etc. Priests must destroy these pagan superstitions.

23. Besides the Ambrosian hymns which we have in canon, we can sing others, which are worthy of this honor and whose author is known.

24. The wars that the Frankish kings wage among themselves must not be a cause of damage to the property of the churches. Anyone (in these wars) who has stolen or confiscated Church property must be required to return it; if he obstinately refuses, he will not only be excommunicated, but also anathematized until his death by all the bishops, who will chant the psalm over him.

25. Is a partial repetition of the 1st canon of the 3rd Councils of Paris, concerning the property of the churches.

26. Judges or powerful people who oppress the poor must be excommunicated if they do not mend their ways after the exhortations of the bishop.

27. It is not only a sacrilegious act, but also even a heretical act, for a bishop to take money from his clerics to confer orders on them; this is what is proven in the book *De dognatibus ecclesiasticis*. Both the one who gave the money and the one who received it, must be excluded from the Church until the next council.

FRANKISH & VISIGOTHIC COUNCILS

3rd Council of Braga (572 AD)
under St. Martin, archbishop of Braga

1. Bishops must visit their dioceses, and ensure that the clerics fulfill their duties exactly, in particular that the catechumens are exorcized twenty days before their baptism, and instructed in the symbol. Bishops must exhort the people to abstain from idolatry and vices.

2. For visiting trips, bishops must only request from each church two solidi. They will not take a third of the oblations and will not ask parish clerics for slave-like services.

3. Orders must be given free of charge.

4. For the small quantity of balsam (chrism) which the bishop gives to the churches to confer baptism no fee can be demanded.

5. The bishop who is asked to consecrate a church must not require anything for this; but he can receive a gift which will be freely given to him. Moreover, he must not consecrate a church if he has not previously seen the document which ensures sufficient endowment.

6. It happened that a church was built by speculation, in order to have half of the offerings that would be made there. No bishop must consecrate such a church.

7. Several people have postponed having their children baptized, due to not being able to pay what was required of them, all these fees are abolished; clerics must not ask for anything for baptism, they can only accept a freely offered gift.

8. He who accuses a cleric of fornication must be able to produce two or three witnesses. If he cannot do this, let him be excommunicated.

9. The metropolitan must indicate to the bishops the date of the Easter feast. On Christmas Day, each cleric must, after the gospel, announce to the people the dates of Lent and Easter. At the beginning of Lent there will be Litany for three days.

10. It is a vestige of Priscillianism when certain priests dared to consecrate masses to the dead, after drinking wine. Anyone in the future who dares to consecrate without fasting will be deposed by the bishop.

FRANKISH & VISIGOTHIC COUNCILS

1st Council of Mâcon (583 AD)
under St. Guntram, King of Orleans

1. Bishops, priests and deacons must not have relations with women who are not their relatives. The grandmother, mother, sister, or niece can stay at home alone, if necessary.

2. No cleric or layman, unless he is of proven virtue and of advanced age, should, without necessity, enter a convent of women; he will not have any secret meetings with the nuns and will only be able to see them in the visiting room. Above all, we must prevent Jews from having access to nuns' convents.

3. No woman should enter the bishop's room unless two priests or deacons are present at the interview.

4. Whoever retains what the dying have given to the Church, will be excommunicated.

5. No cleric must wear secular clothing or shoes, nor carry weapons; if he does so, he will be confined to bread and water for thirty days. The bishop must not say mass without the pallium.

7. If a civil judge seizes or punishes a cleric without the consent of the bishop, except for a capital crime, namely murder, theft or perjury, the judge will be excluded from the Church for as long as the bishop will find it good.

8. No cleric shall cite another before a civil judge. If an inferior cleric does so, he will receive forty lashes minus one; if he belongs to a higher order, he will be locked up for thirty days.

9. From St. Martin's Day until Christmas, we will fast on Monday, Wednesday and Friday of each week. The divine office will be celebrated as in Lent. During this time we must also read the canons, so that no one commits a mistake through ignorance.

10. Clerics must not celebrate feast days without the permission of the bishop.

11. Bishops, priests and clerics who continue to live with their wives must be deposed.

12. A virgin consecrated to God who marries must be excommunicated until her death, as well as the one she marries; if they separate with a true spirit of penitence, the bishop will only keep them excluded from communion for the time he deems sufficient.

13. Jews must not be appointed judges or tax collectors over Christians.

14. From Thursday of Holy Week until Easter, Jews, in accordance with an ordinance of the late King Childebert, must not appear in the streets or in public squares, because they do not act like this to defy Christians. They must show respect to all clerics and must not sit before the priests unless invited to do so.

15. No Christian must, under penalty of excommunication, take part in Jewish meals.

16. No Christian will henceforth be a slave to Jews. If a Jew has a Christian slave, any Christian can buy him from him for twelve solidi, either to free this slave or to take him into his service. If the Jew is dissatisfied and refuses the fixed sum, the Christian slave can go and live wherever he wants with Christians. If a Jew is convicted of having caused one of his Christian slaves to apostatize, he will lose this slave and will be punished according to the laws.

17. Whoever persuades anyone to bear false witness or perjure himself, or who seeks to persuade him to do so, will be excommunicated for the rest of his days. Those who participated in his perjury will no longer be able to bear witness and will be charged with legal infamy.

18. Whoever brings an accusation against innocent people to the judges or to the king will be excommunicated if he is a layman, and if he is a cleric of a higher order, he will be deposed until he has given satisfaction.

19. The nun Agnes gave part of her property to powerful people to ensure their protection, and to be able, by this means, to live as she pleased. She and those who accepted these goods will also be excommunicated.

3rd Council of Lyon (583 AD)
under Priscus, bishop of Lyon

1. Clerics, from the subdiaconate and above, must not have wives in their homes who are not their relatives, and those who are married must not live with their wives.

2. When bishops give letters of recommendation to a poor person, or to a prisoner, the signature must be clearly legible, and it must also indicate how much money the prisoner needs to redeem himself, and what else is necessary for him.

3. Nuns who abandon the convent are excommunicated until their return. However, they will be granted viaticum.

4. On the subject of incestuous unions, the ancient ordinances retain the force of law.

5. Each bishop must celebrate the feasts of Christmas and Easter in his own church, except in cases of illness or the king's order.

6. Lepers in each city must receive food and clothing from their bishop, and they must not go outside to beg.

2nd Council of Mâcon (585 AD)
under St. Guntram, King of Orleans

1. On the sanctification of Sunday.

2. From the solemnity of the Easter festival, which must last six days (from Maundy Thursday until Easter Tuesday exclusively, with the slaves prohibited from working during this time).

3. Except in cases of necessity, no one should be baptized except on Holy Saturday.

4. Every Sunday, the faithful, men and women, must offer the altar bread and wine.

5. The old law stipulating that tithing should be given to the Church is very little observed, and must be put back into force. The tithe is to be used for the benefit of the poor (and the clergy), and to redeem prisoners. Anyone who stubbornly refuses it will be excommunicated forever.

6. We renew the prescription of the Council of Hippo requiring that priests celebrate only on an empty stomach; the remains of the consecrated bread, moistened with wine, will be given to eat on Wednesday or Friday to young children who must also be fasting.

7. Slaves, who have been freed in the church, are placed under the protection of bishops, and any discussion relating to their freedom must be brought before the bishop.

8. The right to asylum must be maintained.

9. It has happened that clerics have been torn from their churches by the civil power and thrown into prison; we must not act like this; against a bishop, any complaint must be brought before the metropolitan, who, in less serious cases, will judge the matter alone or by joining one or two bishops; in more serious cases will leave it to the council to decide.

10. Likewise, no one shall seize a priest, a deacon, or a subdeacon; any action against them must be brought before the bishop.

11. Bishops must exercise hospitality.

12. They must also protect widows and orphans against civil judges; they must not, under penalty of excommunication, decide the affairs of widows and orphans, without having previously informed the bishop so that the archdeacon or a priest can attend the trial and judgment.

13. In episcopal houses there must be no dogs, so that the poor who come to take refuge there are not bitten; bishops are also forbidden to have falcons.

14. The powerful, even those who are part of the king's retinue, must not, under penalty of anathema, plunder the weak, in contempt of all rights.

15. When a layman meets a cleric of a higher degree, he must honor him by bowing: when a cleric and a layman, both on horseback, come to meet, the latter must salute the cleric taking off his hat; if the cleric is on foot and the layman on horseback, the latter must dismount and greet him.

16. The widow of a subdeacon, an exorcist or an acolyte must not remarry, under penalty of being locked up in a convent.

17. While a corpse has not fallen into dust, one should not open the tomb to place another corpse therein; nor should a corpse be placed in a tomb which is

the property of another, without the consent of the master; all under penalty of having to exhume these bodies.

18. Incestuous relationships are forbidden.

19. Clerics must not attend criminal trials or the execution of the condemned.

20. Every three years, all the bishops must meet in council, and the archbishop of Lyon must agree with the king to designate the place of the meeting. Anyone who fails to attend without reason will be excluded from a *charitate fratrum*.

1st Council of Auxerre (585 AD)
under St. Aunarius, bishop of Auxerre

1. On the first of January, no one must, in the manner of the pagans, disguise themselves as a cow (or an old woman) or a deer, or make the diabolical gifts of New Year's Day; but on this day, we must not give more presents than on other days.

2. All priests (who are in the countryside) must, before Epiphany, send messengers to the bishop to learn from him what day Lent begins. They must then, on the feast of the Epiphany, announce this day to the people.

3. It is forbidden to celebrate mass or night vigils on the feasts of saints in private houses; nor should one perform vows near a bush, or a sacred tree, or a spring; but whoever has made a vow, must watch in the church, and fulfill this vow for the benefit of the clerics and for the poor. No one must make images representing men or wooden legs.

4. We must not give ear to soothsayers and sorcerers, no more than to those who explain the future. We must also no longer practice the sorts sanclorum nor pay attention to what we have with wood or with bread.

5. Vigils in honor of Saint Martin are prohibited.

FRANKISH & VISIGOTHIC COUNCILS

6. From the middle of Lent, each priest must ask for chrism. If he cannot come himself due to illness, he must entrust this mission to his archdeacon, or to the archsubdeacon. The chrism must be carried in a chrismarium and in a linen cloth, just like the relics.

7. In the middle of May, all the priests must meet in synod in the city, and on November 1st all the abbots must do the same.

8. Only wine mixed with water should be offered for consecration, and not wine mixed with honey or any other liquid.

9. We must not suffer in the church from worldly choirs or the songs of young girls; we must not eat there either.

10. Two masses must not be said on the same day at the same altar, and when the bishop has said mass at an altar, no other priest must celebrate there on that day.

11. Non licet vigilia Paschse ante or a secunda noctis vigilias perexpedire quia ipsa nocte non licet post media nocte bibere, nec natal Domini, nec reliquas sollemnitates. [It is not permissible to hasten the vigil of the Passover before midnight, because it is not permissible to drink after midnight on the night itself, nor the Nativity of the Lord, nor the other festivals.]

12. The dead should not be given the Eucharist or kisses, nor should their bodies be covered with awnings or palls.

13. The deacon must not place the *peforanilapalle* on his shoulders.

14. No corpses should be buried in baptistery.

15. One must not bury a body on top of another.

16. Work is prohibited on Sunday.

17. It is not permitted to accept offerings in favor of suicides.

18. In certain cases of necessity, one should only baptize at Easter.

19. A priest, or a deacon, or a subdeacon, who has already eaten, must not perform functions at mass, nor must he remain in the church during this mass.

20. When a priest, a deacon, or a subdeacon has committed a carnal sin, and is not denounced to the bishop or the archdeacon by the archpriest, the latter will be excommunicated for one year.

21. Every priest after ordination must no longer share his wife's bed (*presbyter*) nor have carnal intercourse with her. It is the same for the deacon and the subdeacon.

22. The widow of a priest, deacon or subdeacon must no longer marry.

23. When an abbot does not punish a serious fault committed by one of his monks or does not denounce it to the bishop or the archdeacon, he will be punished and sent to another monastery.

24. No abbot or monk should go to weddings.

25. No abbot or monk can be godfather.

26. No abbot should allow a woman to enter his monastery, not even to see a solemnity. If he does, he will be relegated to another monastery and condemned to bread and water for three months.

3rd Council of Toledo (589 AD)
under Reccarded I, King of Visigoths

1. Whoever abides in fellowship with the Arians, and maintains their doctrine, let him be accursed.

2. Whoever does not recognize that the Son of God Our Lord Jesus Christ was begotten of the substance of the Father before all beginning, and that he is equal to him and of the same substance, let him be anathema.

3. Whoever refuses to believe that the Holy Spirit proceeds from the Father and the Son and is equally eternal and equal to the Father and the Son, let him be accursed.

4. Whoever does not distinguish the persons in the Trinity, let him be accursed.

5. Whoever declares the Son and the Holy Spirit less than the Father, let him be accursed.

6. Whoever does not admit that the Father, the Son and the Holy Spirit have the same substance, the same omnipotence and the same eternity, let him be anathema.

7. Whoever believes that the Son does not know anything, let him be accursed.

8. Whoever attributes a beginning to the Son and the Holy Spirit, let him be accursed.

9. Whoever believes that the Son was visible and capable of suffering as to his divinity, let him be accursed.

10. Whoever does not consider the Holy Spirit to be true and almighty God, as well as the Father and the Son, let him be accursed.

11. Whoever declares a faith other than that of Nicaea, Constantinople, Ephesus, and Chalcedon Catholic, let him be accursed.

12. Whoever separates the Father, the Son, and the Holy Spirit in the matter of magnificence and divinity, let him be accursed.

13. Whoever believes that the Son and the Holy Spirit are not to be worshiped equally with the Father, let him be accursed.

14. Whoever does not say: Gloria et honor Patri et Filio et Spiritui sancto, let him be anathema.

15. Whoever forbids or practices the second baptism, let him be accursed.

16. Whoever approves of the detestable writings which we published in the twelfth year of the reign of Leovigild to convert the Romans to Arianism, let him be anathema.

17. Whoever does not reject, in the most formal manner, the Council of Rimini, let him be anathema.

18. We recognize that we have most explicitly left the heresy of Arius, to attach ourselves to the Catholic Church. We profess the faith which our king professed before the council, and we want to teach it to our faithful. Let him to whom this faith displeases be anathema.

19-22. Whoever rejects the faith of the councils of Nicaea, Constantinople, Ephesus and Chalcedon, let him be accursed.

23. We sign with our own hand this condemnation of Arian errors. We subscribe to the definitions of each of these councils of Nicaea, Constantinople, Ephesus and Chalcedon; they explicitly contain the Orthodox doctrine on the Trinity and the Incarnation. May he who alters this holy doctrine, and separates himself from the Catholic communion, to which we have joined, be responsible before God and before the world.

FRANKISH & VISIGOTHIC COUNCILS

1st Council of Narbonne (589 AD)
under Migetius, Archbishop of Narbonne

1. No cleric must wear a purple habit; this is suitable for princes and not for religious people.

2. After each psalm, we must sing the Gloria Patri, etc.; psalms that are too long must be divided and Gloria Patri said after each division.

3. No clerc must park in the public square (because of the danger of dissipation).

4. Imposes abstention from servile works on Sunday, under penalty of fine or corporal punishment.

5. According to the 18th canon of Chalcedon (wrongly designated as the canon of Nicaea), clerics are forbidden to enter into conspiracies; prohibition for clerics of a lower degree to offend clerics of a higher degree.

6. When a cleric, or a notable person of the city, is locked up in a convent for some misdeed, the abbot must treat him in accordance with the prescriptions of the bishop.

7. A cleric who acts in a manner contrary to the interests of the Church will be deposed.

8. It will be the same if he usurps the property of the Church.

9. Jews must bury their deceased according to ancient Jewish custom and without singing.

10. Every cleric must remain in the diocese for which he was ordained.

11. Anyone who ignores the letters cannot be ordained a priest or deacon. If he is already ordained, and if he does not want to learn to read and perform the divine office, he will not receive instructions until he has learned it well. If he is stubborn, he will be locked up in a convent.

12. No priest or deacon must leave the altar during the celebration of Mass; no deacon, subdeacon or lector must leave at dawn before the end of mass.

13. Subdeacons, doorkeepers and other servants of the church must discharge their duties diligently. They must lift the hangings which are at the doors, to allow passage to the clerics of a higher degree. If they do not do this, and persist in their negligence, the subdeacons will be punished with a fine, as for the others, they will be beaten.

14. Witchcraft is prohibited.

15. It is also forbidden to celebrate Thursday in the manner of the pagans.

2nd Council of Caesaraugusta (592 AD)
under Artemius, bishop of Caesaraugusta

1. When an Arian priest becomes a Catholic, if he has a pure faith and if he is of good morals, he can be ordained a priest again. It will be the same for deacon.

2. Relics found in Arian churches must be presented by the priests to the bishop and tested by fire.

3. Churches consecrated as Catholic by Arian bishops before their reordination must be rededicated.

Council of Barcelona (599 AD)
Under Asiaticus, archbishop of Barcelona

1. Neither the bishop nor the clerics must ask anything for the collation of orders, or for the installation of a cleric.

2. Nor should we ask for anything for chrism.

3. No layman should be ordained bishop unless he has passed through the intermediate orders and remained there for the time prescribed by the ancient canons. If the clergy and the people have elected and presented to the metropolitan and his colleagues in the episcopate two or three candidates, that one will be sacred on whom the choice of the bishops will fall after they have prepared themselves by fasting.

4. A virgin who has left the habit of the world to take that of religious persons, and who has made a profession of chastity, must no longer marry. It is the same for the one who has received the *benedictio pœnitentiae*.

Council of Tarragona (615 AD)
under Eusebius, bishop of Tarragona

1. The ancient canons must be observed in everything.

2. After the death of a bishop, only the one must be ordained as his successor who has been chosen by the metropolitan and the other bishops of the province, by the clergy and the people of the city, without there being had simony*.

3 (formerly 2). No bishop must choose a successor for himself, and during his life no one must claim to take his place under any pretext, nor be ordained, unless it has been recognized that the bishop is in the absolute impossibility of governing the Church and the clergy.

4. Unanimously we decided that if a bishop, which has never happened, deposes an abbot in a non-canonical manner, this abbot must petition the council; If in the meantime the bishop dies, his successor must restore the abbot to his seat 1.

5 (formerly 3). No cleric, whatever the dignity with which he is invested, can leave aside his bishop (*conlempto episcopa*) nor turn to princes or the powerful to obtain their support. The latter should not listen to him, unless he is willing

to ask for forgiveness (from the bishop). Anyone who acts otherwise will be punished in accordance with the ancient canons 2.

6 (formerly 4). No secular judge should punish a cleric without the knowledge of his bishop. If he does so, he will be excluded from the Church until he understands his fault and mends his ways.

7 (formerly 5). Freedmen are under the protection of the Church and must no longer be claimed for tax purposes. Anyone who seeks to regain their freedom, demands for the tax and is deaf to the bishop's reprimands, will be excommunicated.

8 (formerly 6). What has been founded for the maintenance of churches must be administered in accordance with the will of the donor, by the bishop or the priest, or by the clerics who serve this church. Anyone who takes anything from this income will be excommunicated.

9 (formerly 7). When a bishop or other cleric dies, one must not, even by virtue of an order from the king or the civil judge, touch the ecclesiastical or private property that he has left behind; but the archdeacon or the clergy must manage these goods, until the stipulations of the testaments are known. Anyone who acts otherwise will be excluded from communion as a murderer of the poor.

10 (formerly 8). The archbishop and the archdeacon must not, as has often happened hitherto, take for themselves, or for their church, what an abbot, or a priest, or another servant of the church has left to another church (titulus); but he must faithfully hand over this inheritance to the very church to which it was given by the dying person.

11 (formerly 9). No bishop or lay person should claim or receive from anyone, or possess the property of another bishop (whether ecclesiastical or private property), under the pretext that it is necessary to defend the kingdom, or there is a (new) division of the provinces.

12 (formerly 10). The wills of bishops and other clerics by which they make donations to the church, or to any person, must be valid, even if they are not entirely in conformity with the prescriptions of civil law.

13 (formerly 11). When a bishop has a lawsuit with another bishop, he must discuss it before the metropolitan, and not before a civil judge.

14 (formerly 12). No monk or nun (*monacha*) must withdraw from his convent under penalty of excommunication until his deathbed.

15. (old 13). Virgins and widows who, remaining in their house, have taken up the religious habit, or who have received it from their parents, must not marry.

16 (formerly 14). Incestuous marriages are prohibited.

17 (former 15) No Jew should have power over Christians, military or civilian. If he exercises one, he will be baptized as well as his family.

The Scriptorium Project is the work of a small group of lay people of various apostolic churches who are interested in the preservation, transmission, and translation of the works of the early and medieval church. Our efforts are to make the works of the church fathers accessible to anyone who might have an interest in Christian antiquities and the theological, philosophical, and moral writings that have become the bedrock of Western Civilization.

To-date, our releases have pulled from the Greek, Syriac, Georgian, Latin, Celtic, Ethiopian, and Coptic traditions of Christianity, and have been pulled from sundry local traditions and languages.

Other Selections from the Early Frankish Church Series:

Frankish & Visigothic Councils: 549-615 AD (June 2007)
Letter to Brunhilda of Austrasia by St. Germain of Paris (Sept. 2010)
The Spiritual Combat by St. Bernard of Clairvaux (Dec. 2010)
In Praise of the New Chivalry by St. Bernard of Clairvaux (Jan. 2011)
Testament by St. Burgundofara the Abbess (Jan. 2016)
Laws of the Monastery and the Church by Theuderic III, King of Franks (Feb. 2016)
The Life of King Sigebert II by Sigebert of Gembloux (Mar. 2016)
Two Letters from a Gallic Patrician by Dynamius the Patrician (July 2016)
Life of St. Germain by St. Venantius Fortunatus (Aug. 2016)
Three Letters from the Companion of the Bulgars by St. Rupert of Juvavum (Aug. 2017)
An Account of the Gallican Liturgy by St. Germain of Paris (June 2018)
Preludes by Photius of Paris (Nov. 2018)
The Privileges of Rome by Louis I the Pious, Frankish Emperor (Apr. 2019)
Edicts of the Synod of Paris by Chlothar II, King of Franks (Aug. 2019)
Laws of the Church (Ecclesiasticae Praeceptiones) by Chlothar III, King of Franks (Apr. 2020)
Laws of the Church (Ecclesiasticae Praeceptiones) by St. Dagobert II, King of Franks (Sept. 2020)
Letters of Paulinus by St. Paulinus of Aquileia (Aug. 2021)
The Italian Diplomas by Charlemagne, Holy Roman Emperor (Apr. 2023)

www.ingramcontent.com/pod-product-compliance
Lightning Source LLC
LaVergne TN
LVHW012048070526
838201LV00082B/3852